5D Consciousness Activations

"The Great Remembering of Humanity."

LMM

5DLIFENOW

5D Consciousness Activations

*"The Great Remembering
of Humanity"*

Volume 2

**11/11/22
Updated 23/05/23**

Dedication
This book is dedicated to my husband, three Earth Human children and ten Essasani Grey-Human Hybrid children.

**Compiled by L. M. M.
5dlifenow@gmail.com
5dlifenow.ca
5DLIFENOW**

5D Consciousness Activations

"The Great Remembering of Humanity"

Table of Contents

The information in this book has been kept hidden from humanity throughout time. We needed to evolve to the point where we are now to be able to comprehend it all and use our powers wisely. We reached that point December 21st, 2012.

It was also suppressed because of outside influences that still want to control and continue to take advantage of humanity.

By reading this, you are taking a step forward in unlocking the remaining 90% of your highly advanced DNA and neurological pathways. And, to help set us free from any negative outside influences.

The foundational piece of 5D consciousness is that everything is energy starting at the 1D atomic level.

Each of the dimensions are layered on top of each other, just as this diagram shows each part flows into the next.

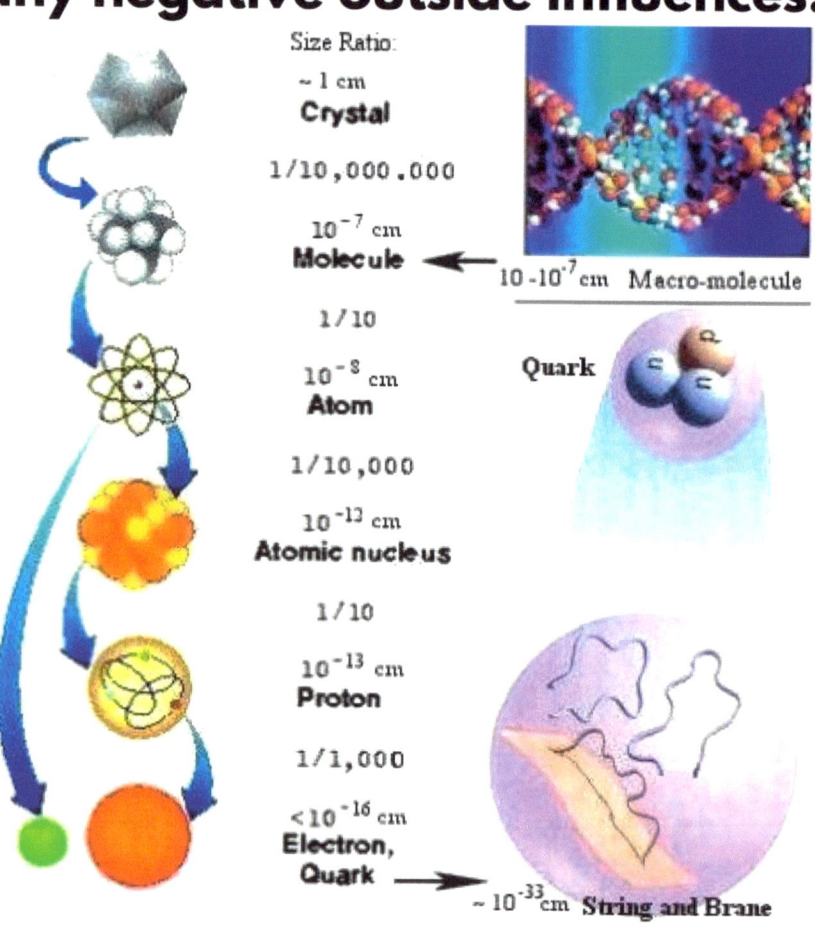

Size Ratio:

~ 1 cm
Crystal

1/10,000.000

10^{-7} cm
Molecule ← $10 - 10^{-7}$ cm Macro-molecule

1/10

10^{-8} cm
Atom

Quark

1/10,000

10^{-12} cm
Atomic nucleus

1/10

10^{-13} cm
Proton

1/1,000

$<10^{-16}$ cm
Electron, Quark →

~ 10^{-33} cm **String and Brane**

The Great Remembering of humanity has marked the official beginning of a quantum evolutionary leap into 5D cosmic consciousness.

The images, visuals, charts and graphics are used as 5D activations to expand your consciousness.

Take a deep breath and step into your true power through these activations.

Everything including your body is made up of divine energy shown here in the Higgs Boson "God Particle". This is the divine creator's essence in and connected into literally everything. And yes, everything has some level of consciousness.

Throughout this book, you'll discover the keys to unlocking your divine pathway forward into higher levels of consciousness.

If you feel guided to, say this strongly and out loud three times:

"I am now activating my higher 5D consciousness smoothly, divinely, lovingly, and standing strong in my highest most beneficial timeline."

By you saying this you're also updating the social memory complex systems of humanity.

As you know, we're all energy, our thoughts and emotions are electromagnetic, each sends out a signal that creates a tiny thought cloud.

When two or more people think and feel the same vibration energy it becomes an egregore. When mass amounts of people think and feel the same emotions they become The Social Memory Complex. It's quantum stored etheric information that we are all connected into together through the Cosmic Web.

This book is of remembering, who we are and is to be used as a consciousness guide to help you along your journey into 5th dimensional life of the new earth.

Congratulations, you made it! Now let's dive into activating your higher consciousness.

Humans have 2 bodies; the physical and energetic. When fully activated humans can create a Merkabah Light Body Vessel.

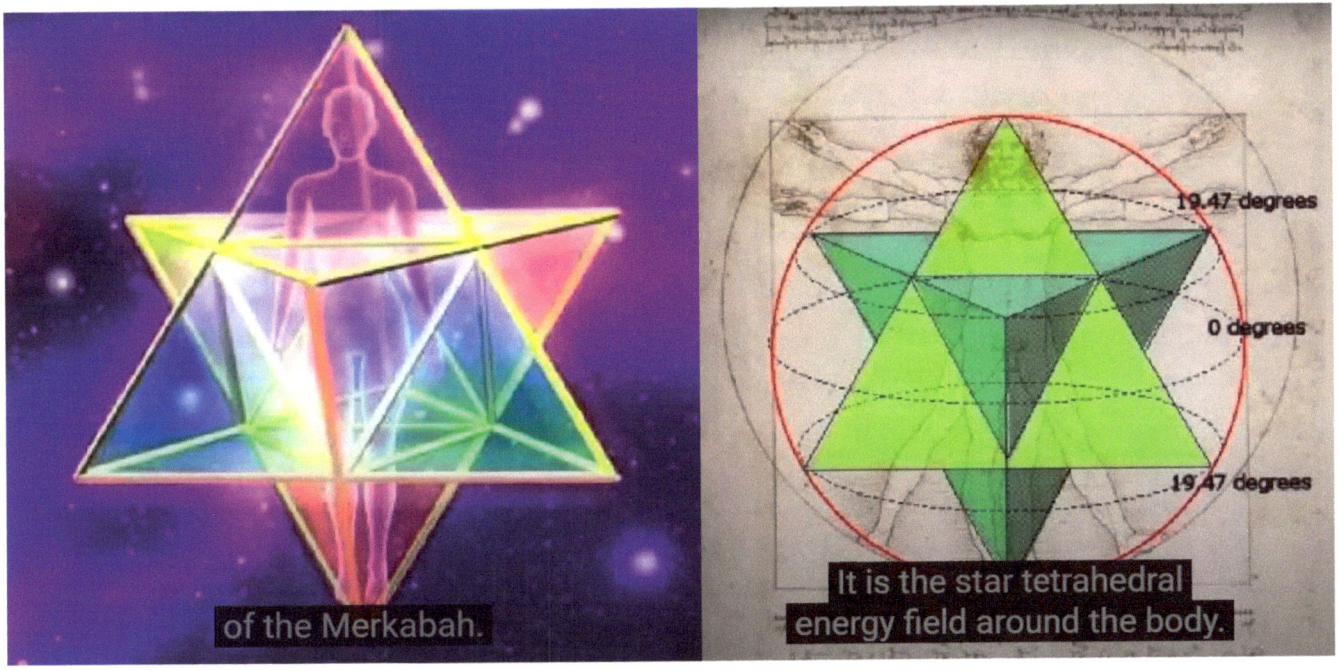

of the Merkabah.

19.47 degrees

0 degrees

19.47 degrees

It is the star tetrahedral energy field around the body.

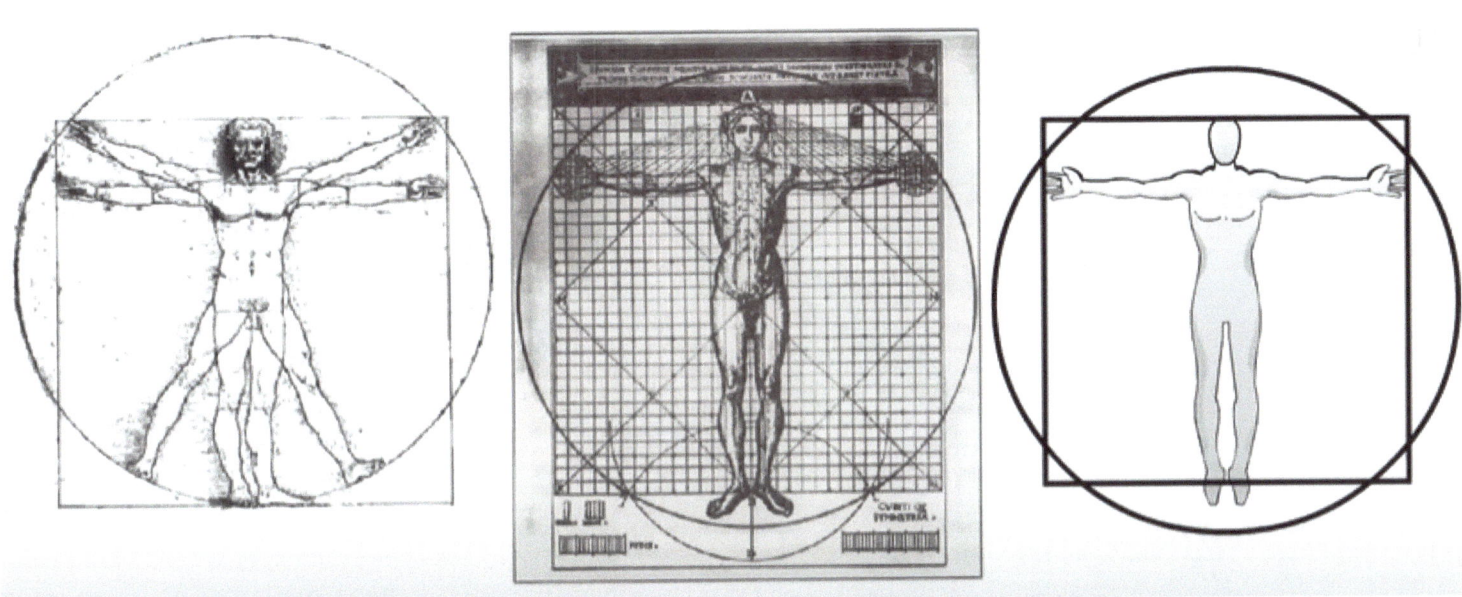

Tip: Spirit Science has excellent information and visual explanations of Merkabas.

Our energetic body connects completely through our physical body and has energy centers that move the flow of energy called Chakras.

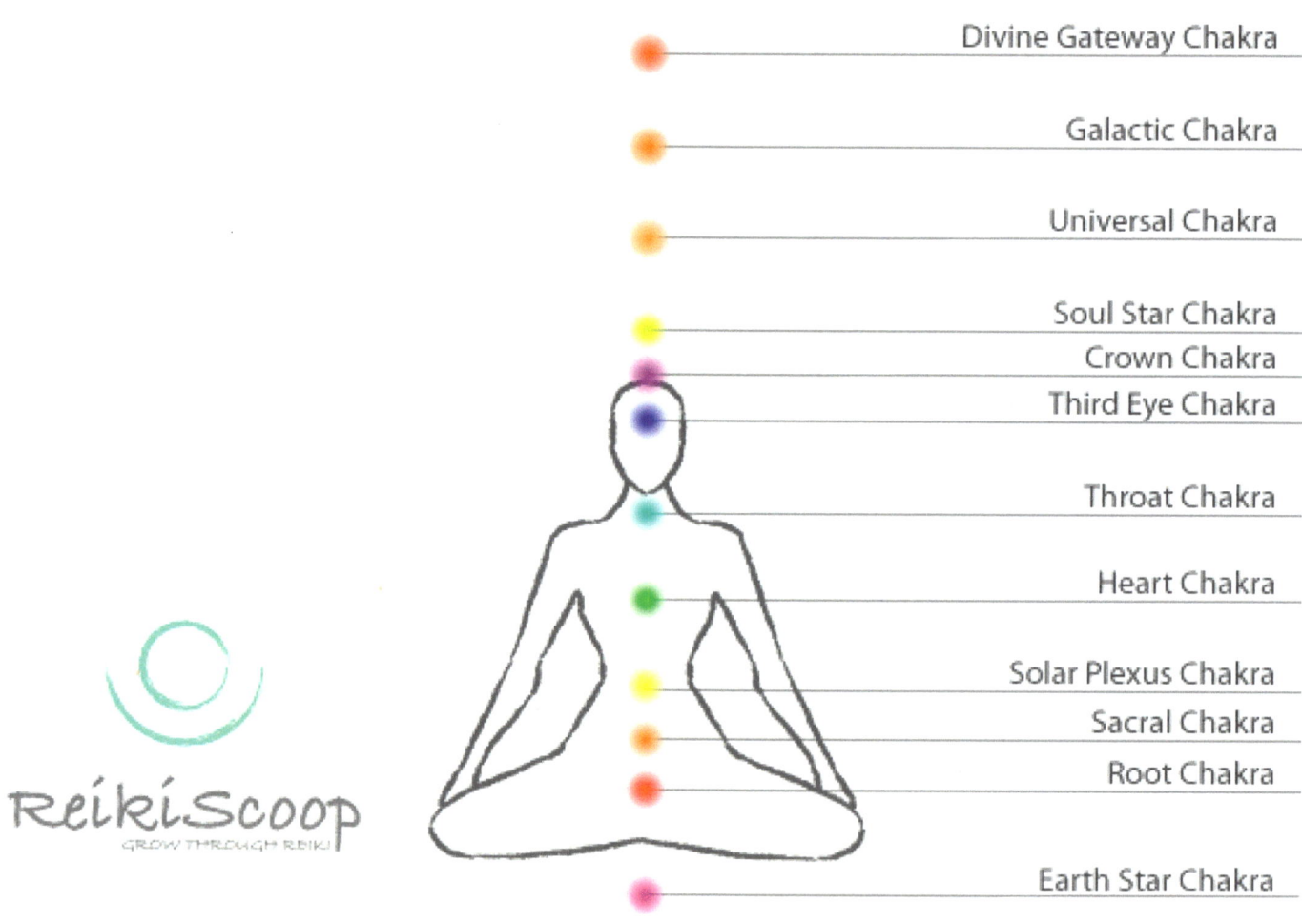

Divine Gateway Chakra

Galactic Chakra

Universal Chakra

Soul Star Chakra
Crown Chakra
Third Eye Chakra

Throat Chakra

Heart Chakra

Solar Plexus Chakra
Sacral Chakra
Root Chakra

Earth Star Chakra

ReikiScoop
GROW THROUGH REIKI

Tip: when breathing in, imagine each of the chakras lighting up and spinning clockwise starting from the bottom up clearing any stagnent energy away.

This is the Human Toroidal or Torus Field made up of the energy that is constantly moving through and around each individual person at all times. Your heart has a toroidal field too. Connect in with yours intentionally right now just by thinking of it and imagining it.

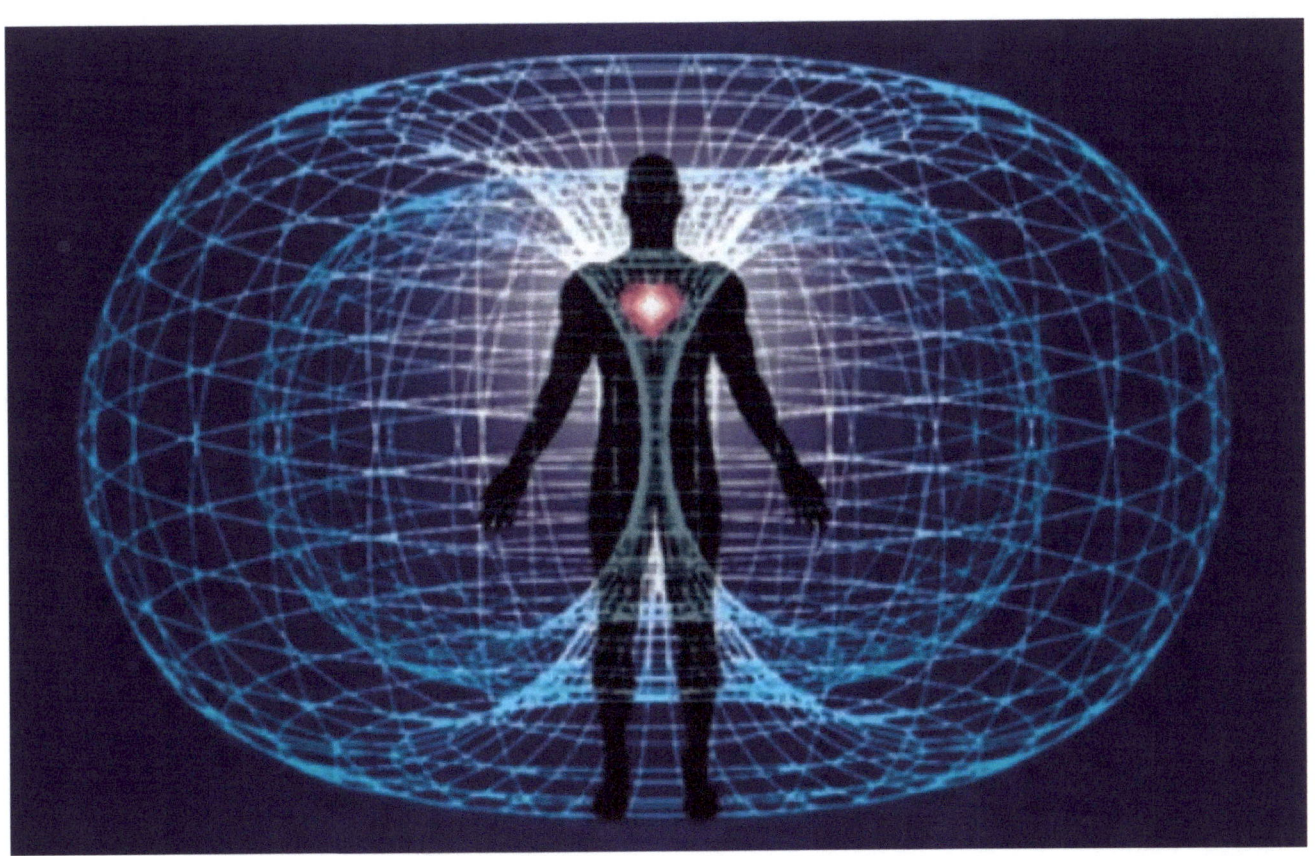

In fact, everything has a torus field. We have the ability to connect into other people or object's fields and can alter them intentionally or unintentionally. Tap into your field or as many people say "bubble".

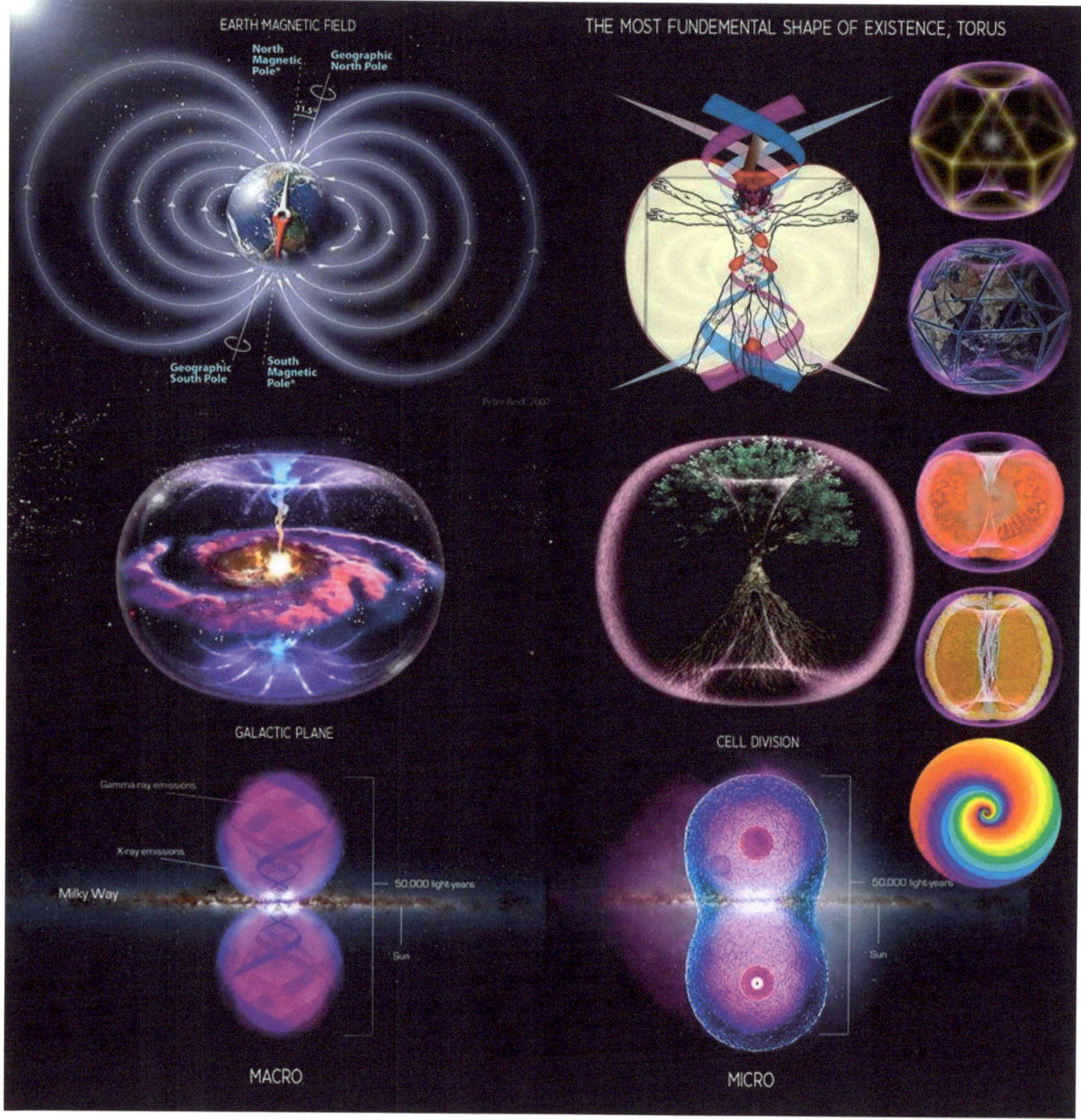

Just like the layers of our skin and parts of our physical body, there are many layers to our energetic bodies too.

Universal Life Force Currents form and sustain the "Auric Field" Levels of 15-Dimensional Human Anatomy
Auric Level, Chakra and Hova Body Correspondences

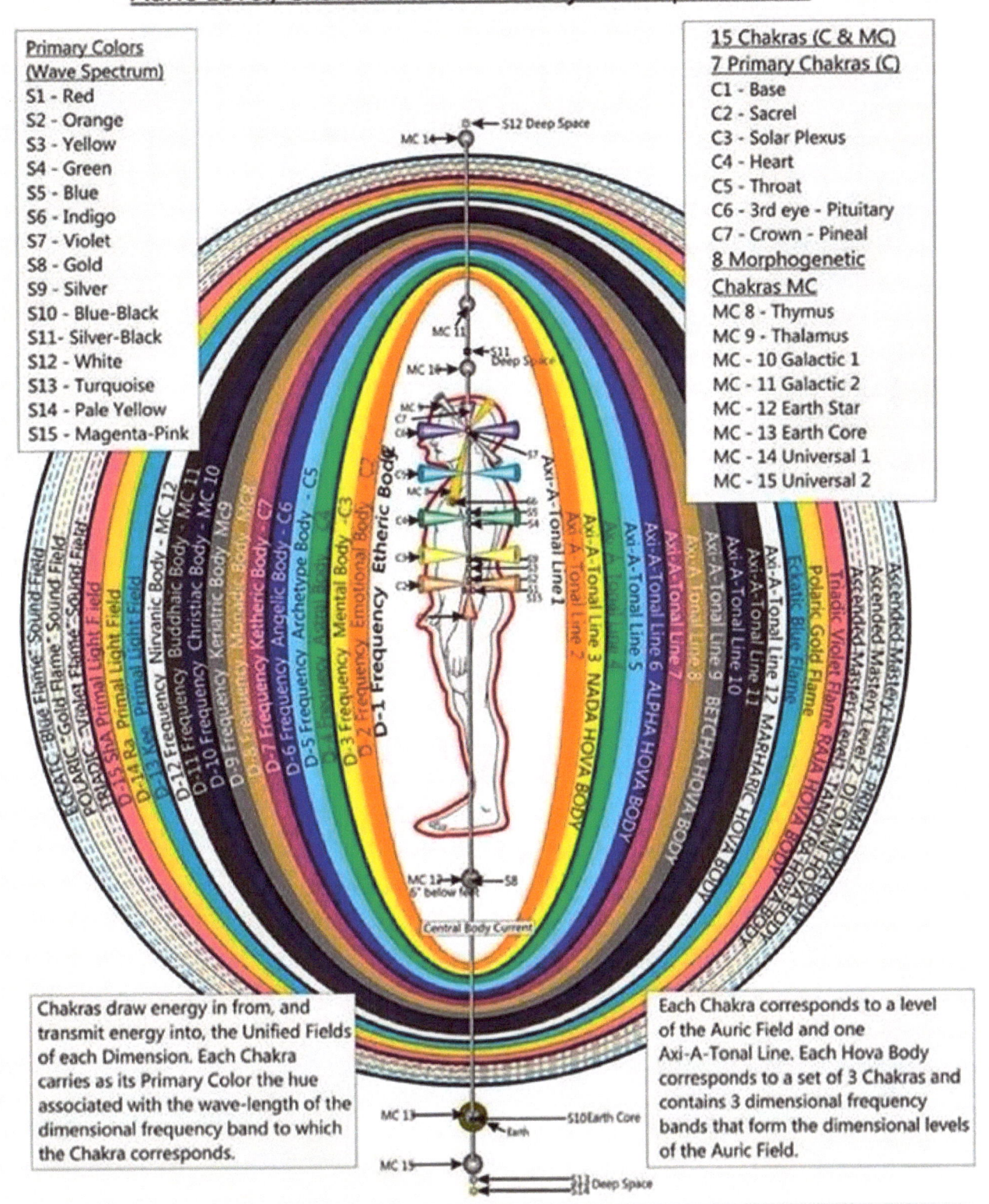

Primary Colors (Wave Spectrum)
S1 - Red
S2 - Orange
S3 - Yellow
S4 - Green
S5 - Blue
S6 - Indigo
S7 - Violet
S8 - Gold
S9 - Silver
S10 - Blue-Black
S11- Silver-Black
S12 - White
S13 - Turquoise
S14 - Pale Yellow
S15 - Magenta-Pink

15 Chakras (C & MC)
7 Primary Chakras (C)
C1 - Base
C2 - Sacral
C3 - Solar Plexus
C4 - Heart
C5 - Throat
C6 - 3rd eye - Pituitary
C7 - Crown - Pineal
8 Morphogenetic Chakras MC
MC 8 - Thymus
MC 9 - Thalamus
MC - 10 Galactic 1
MC - 11 Galactic 2
MC - 12 Earth Star
MC - 13 Earth Core
MC - 14 Universal 1
MC - 15 Universal 2

Chakras draw energy in from, and transmit energy into, the Unified Fields of each Dimension. Each Chakra carries as its Primary Color the hue associated with the wave-length of the dimensional frequency band to which the Chakra corresponds.

Each Chakra corresponds to a level of the Auric Field and one Axi-A-Tonal Line. Each Hova Body corresponds to a set of 3 Chakras and contains 3 dimensional frequency bands that form the dimensional levels of the Auric Field.

Our brain emits waves of frequency and our thoughts are electromagnetic, which can all be measured. Dr. Joe Dispenza and Dr. Silva are excellent teachers in the field of harnessing brain wave power for healing, genius level learning and much more.

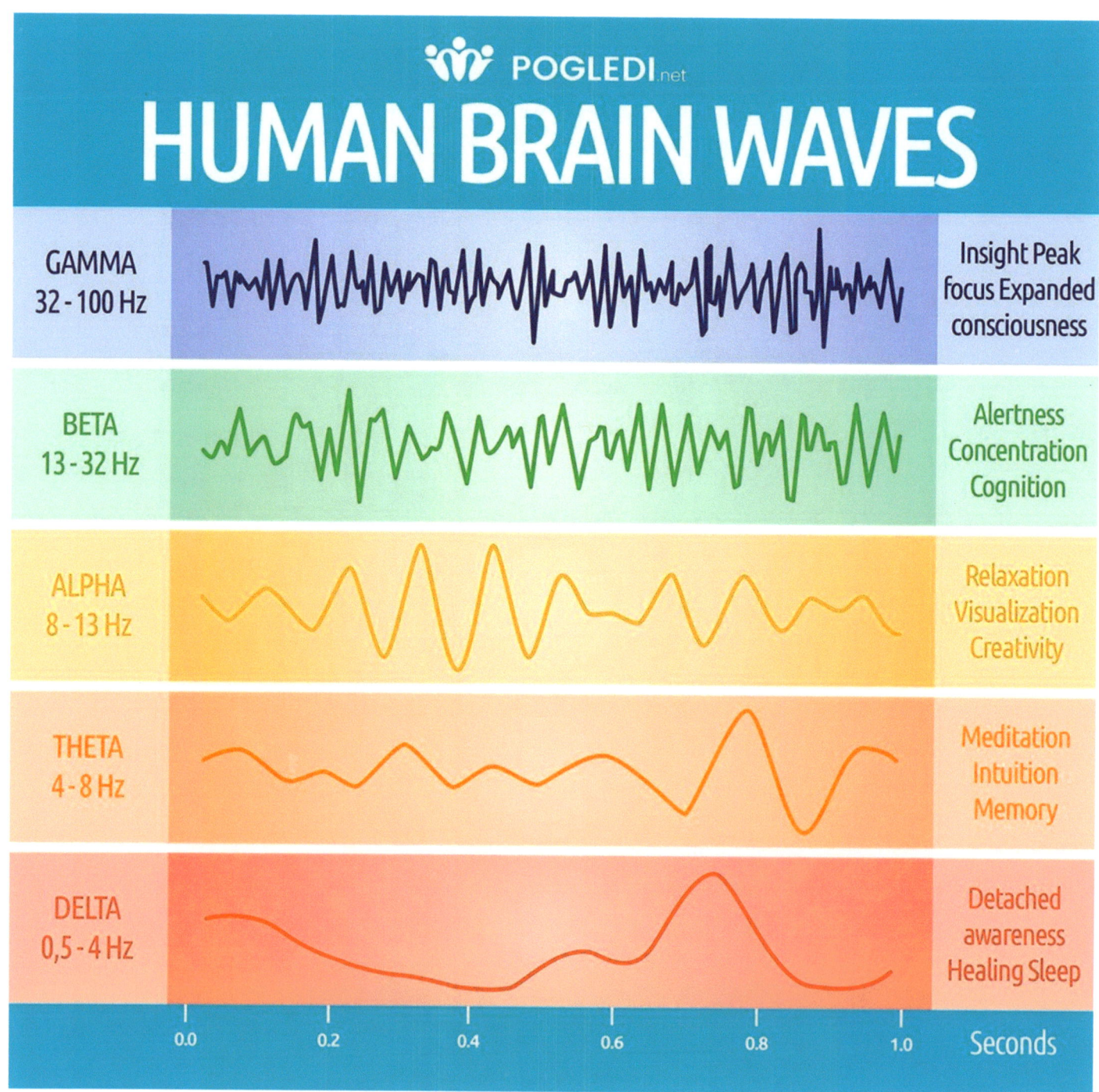

The human brain works similarly to a computer. The memories and thoughts are stored in electric neurological pathways and in the energetic body too. The Reticular Activating System or RAS is the human brain's filtering system. It deems what information is important and what is not.

The human brain can only process a fraction of information our eyes see. It filters out information that isn't in its programming. So, a person could see true information but because of their programming their brain will typically reject and ignore it.

Are you consciously aware of your RAS programming?

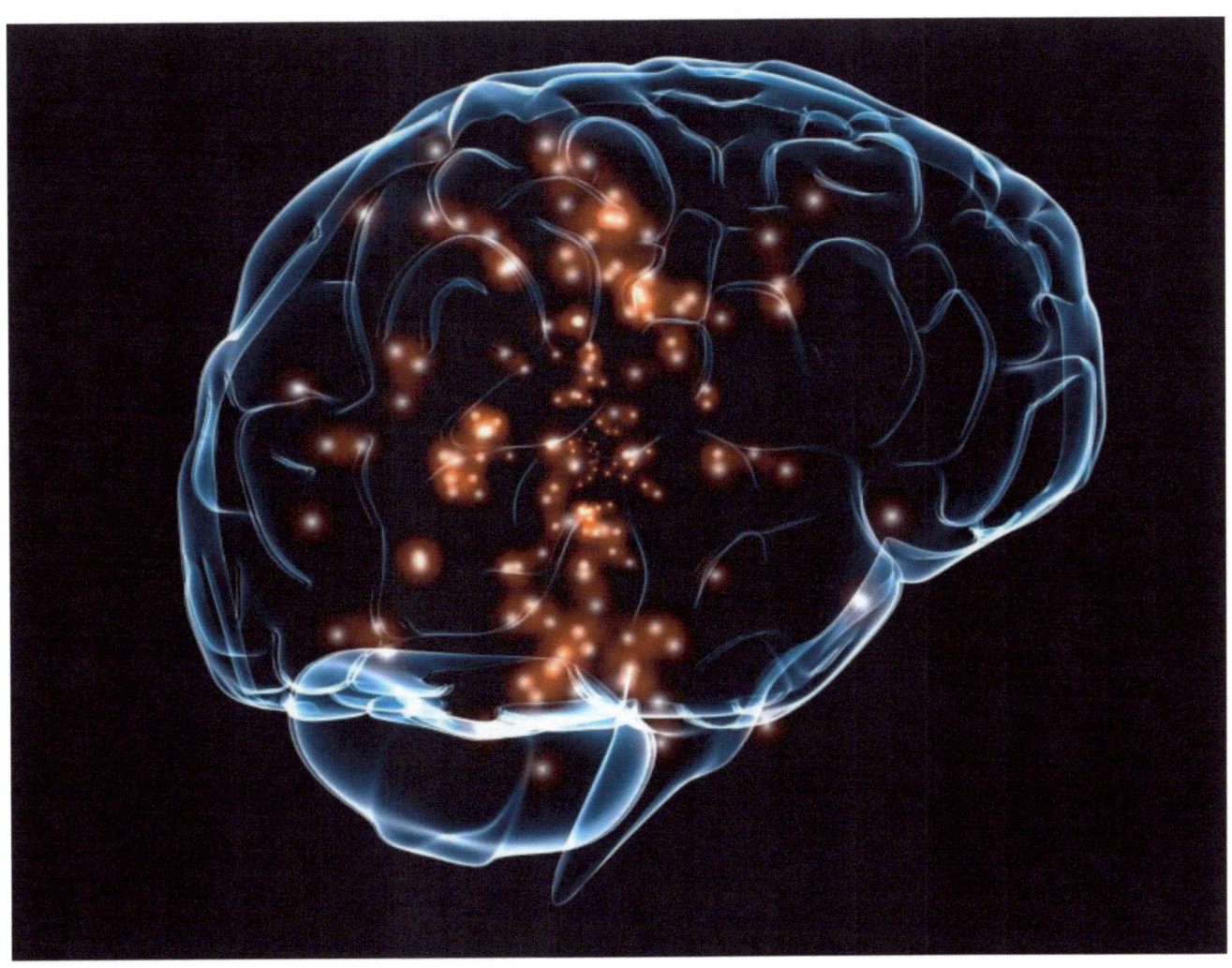

Check into your body's frequency. Where are you at?

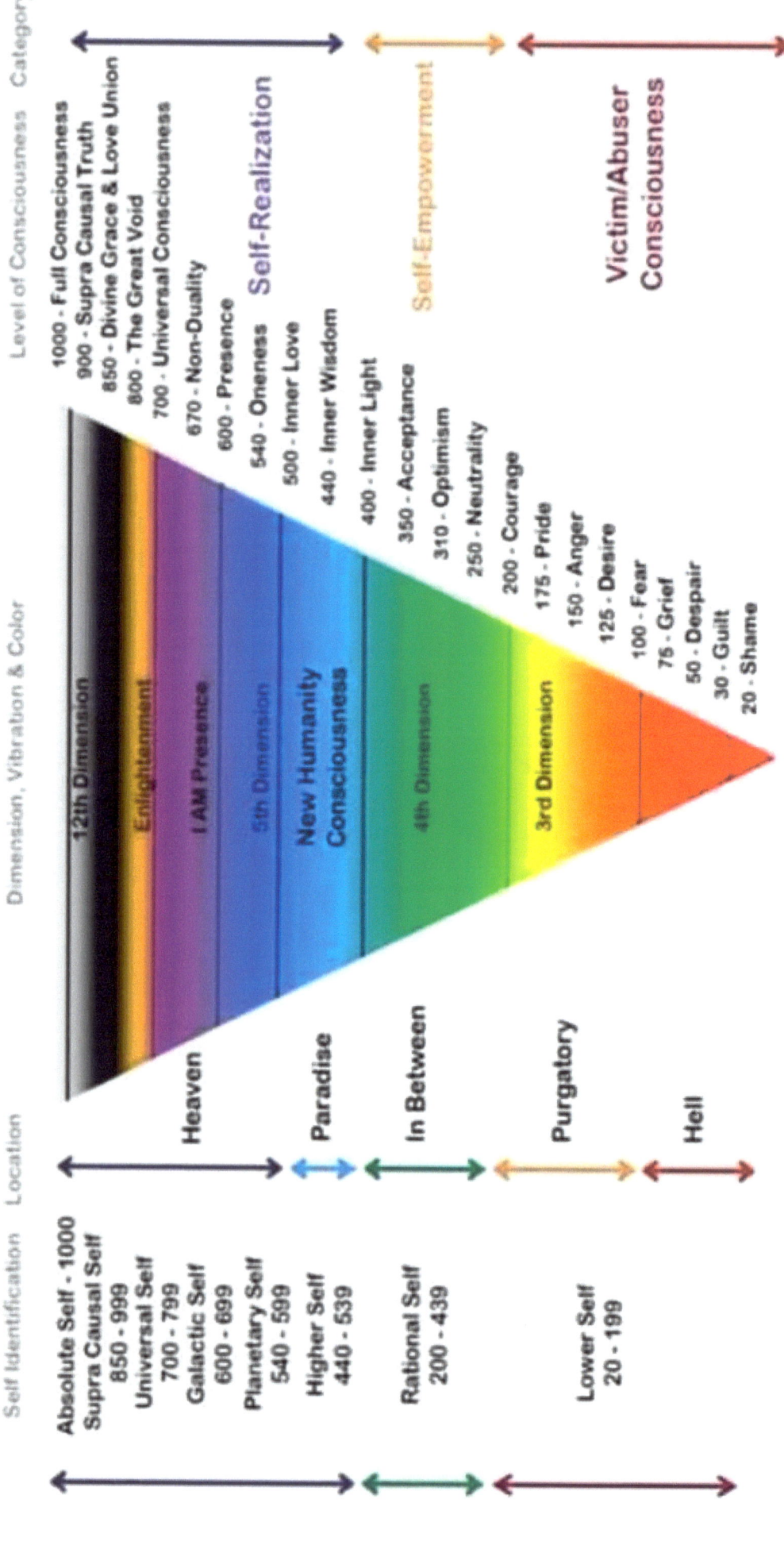

Map of Consciousness Levels

from David R. Hawkins   *Power vs. Force*

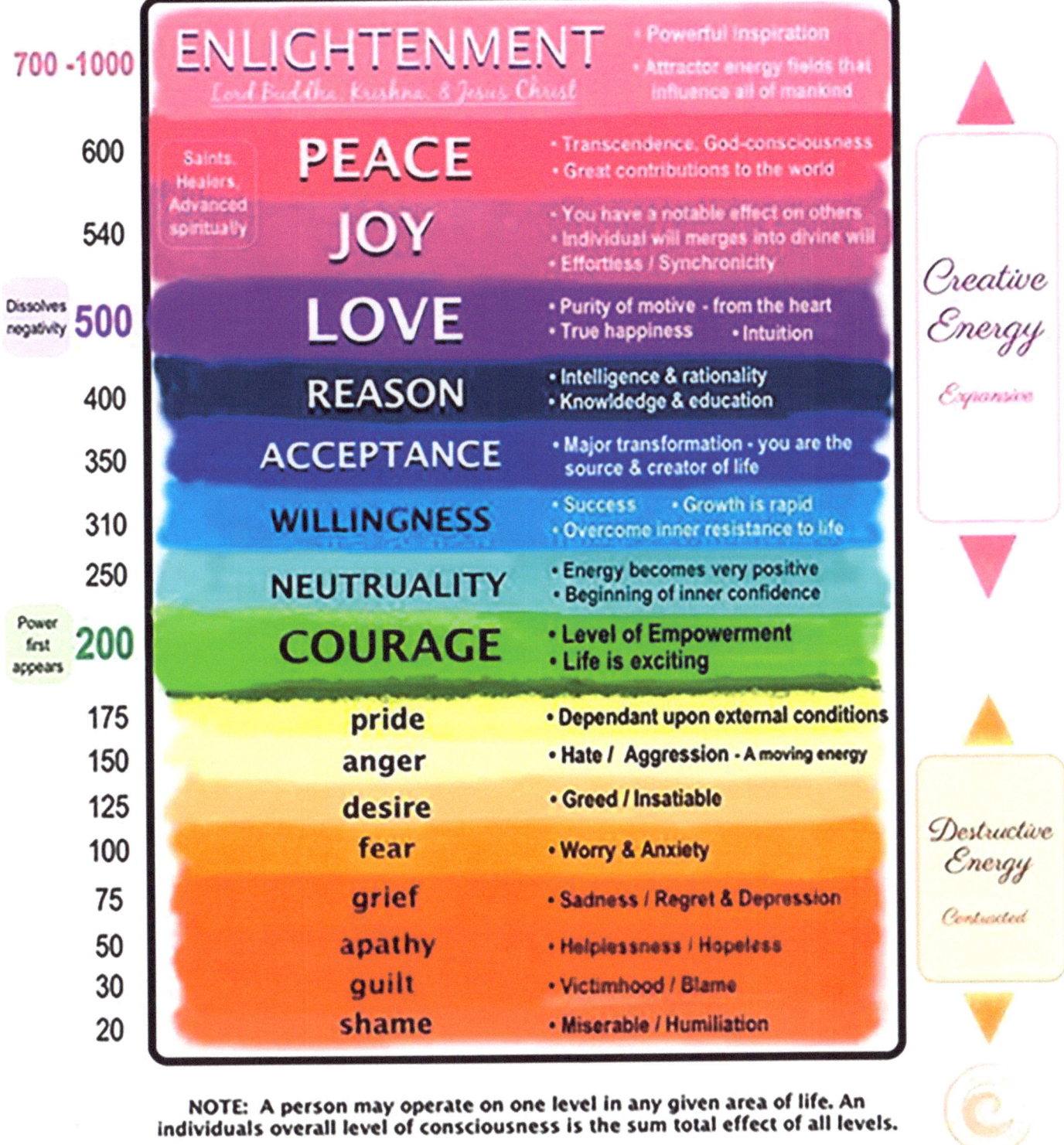

700 -1000	**ENLIGHTENMENT** *Lord Buddha, Krishna, & Jesus Christ*	• Powerful Inspiration • Attractor energy fields that influence all of mankind
600	*Saints, Healers, Advanced spiritually* **PEACE**	• Transcendence, God-consciousness • Great contributions to the world
540	**JOY**	• You have a notable effect on others • Individual will merges into divine will • Effortless / Synchronicity
Dissolves negativity 500	**LOVE**	• Purity of motive - from the heart • True happiness • Intuition
400	**REASON**	• Intelligence & rationality • Knowledge & education
350	**ACCEPTANCE**	• Major transformation - you are the source & creator of life
310	**WILLINGNESS**	• Success • Growth is rapid • Overcome inner resistance to life
250	**NEUTRUALITY**	• Energy becomes very positive • Beginning of inner confidence
Power first appears 200	**COURAGE**	• Level of Empowerment • Life is exciting
175	pride	• Dependant upon external conditions
150	anger	• Hate / Aggression - A moving energy
125	desire	• Greed / Insatiable
100	fear	• Worry & Anxiety
75	grief	• Sadness / Regret & Depression
50	apathy	• Helplessness / Hopeless
30	guilt	• Victimhood / Blame
20	shame	• Miserable / Humiliation

Creative Energy Expansive

Destructive Energy Contracted

NOTE: A person may operate on one level in any given area of life. An individuals overall level of consciousness is the sum total effect of all levels.

A main soul mission that all light beings have is to raise the vibration of themselves, humanity and the planet. By intentionally being in a higher vibrational resonance you contribute to raising it for the benefit of all while aligning yourself to your highest timeline.

EASY WAYS TO RAISE YOUR VIBRATION

@HEALINGFACTS

1. Repeat positive affirmations to yourself daily.
2. Start to appreciate the present moment more.
3. Eat high vibrational foods, like fruits and herbs.
4. Hydrate and flush out toxins with distilled water.
5. Meditate everyday and devote yourself to a daily practice.
6. Movement increases vibration; dance, stretch, flow, hike!
7. Listen to healing frequencies (528 Hz, 432 Hz, etc)
8. Devote time to hobbies that make you genuinely happy.
9. Spend time in nature and express gratitude to the Earth.
10. Consume less, give more!

We have only been told, taught and shown the lowest three dimensions of ourselves and the universe. There is so much more for us to discover!

Universal Templar Complex: Spheres within Spheres

15-Dimensional Time Matrix
5 Density Universes (DU)

Yunasai
Source-GOD
Exists beyond the Time Matrix

Particle Universe
Particum, Base Magnetic, Vibration

Khundaray — Life Force Energy
3 Primal Sound Fields
Kee-Ra-ShA — Life Force Energy
3 Primal Light Fields
Maharata — Life Force Energy — Dimensions 10-12
Kundalini — Life Force Energy — Dimensions 1-9

5 Density Universes

ECKATIC LEVEL		Cosmic Mind
POLARIC LEVEL		Cosmic Mind
TRIADIC LEVEL		Cosmic Mind

Ascended Masters — D15 — Partika Mind — Violet Flame
Ascended Masters — D14 — Partiki Mind — Gold Flame
Ascended Masters — D13 — Particum Mind — Blue Flame
Rishi — D12 — Nirvanic Mind — D12 Divine Blueprint
Rishi — D11 — Buddhaic Mind
Rishi — D10 — Christiac Mind
Christos Avatars — D9 — Keriatic Mind
Avatars — D8 — Monadic Mind — "Archangels"
Avatars — D7 — Ketheric Mind — "Archangels"
Over Souls — D6 — Celestial Mind — "Archangels"
Over Souls — D5 — Archetype Mind — "Angels"
Over Souls — D4 — Astral Mind
Souls — D3 — Earth — Reasoning Mind
Souls — D2 — Incarnates — Instinctual Mind
Souls — D1 — DU-1 Carbon Matter — Subconscious Mind

DU-2 Carbon-Etheric Matter — Tara
DU-3 Etheric Matter — Gaia — Adjacent Earths
DU-4 Hydroplasmic Pre-Matter — Aramatena
DU-5 Ante-Matter

Energy Matrix

D4, D5, D6, D7, D8, D9, D10, D11, D12, D13, D14, D15

Density Universe (3 dimensions)
Dimension — 26,556 years / 8,852 years
Continuum — 4,426 years

Anti-Particle Universe (Parallel)
Partika, Base Electric, Oscillation

3 Primal Light Fields

Rishi — D15
Rishi — D14
Rishi — D13
Avatars — D12
Avatars — D11
Avatars — D10
Over Souls — D9
Over Souls — D8
Over Souls — D7
Souls — D6
Souls — D5
Souls — D4
D3
D2 — Incarnates
DU-1 Carbon Matter — D1 — Parallel Earth — Parallel Inner Earth
DU-2 Non-Etheric Matter — Parallel Tara
D3, D4, D5, D6, D7, D8, D9, D10, D11, D12, D13, D14, D15

"Pit"
Phantom Matrix Anomaly
Black Hole Sub-Time Distortion Cycle

Avatars — D11.5
Avatars — D11
Avatars — D10
Over Souls — D9
Over Souls — D8
Over Souls — D7
Souls — D6
Souls — D5
Souls — D4
D3
D2 — Incarnates
D1 — Phantom Earth
D3, D4, D5, D6, D7, D8, D9, D10, D11, D11.5

www. CHRISTOS AVATAR .com

14

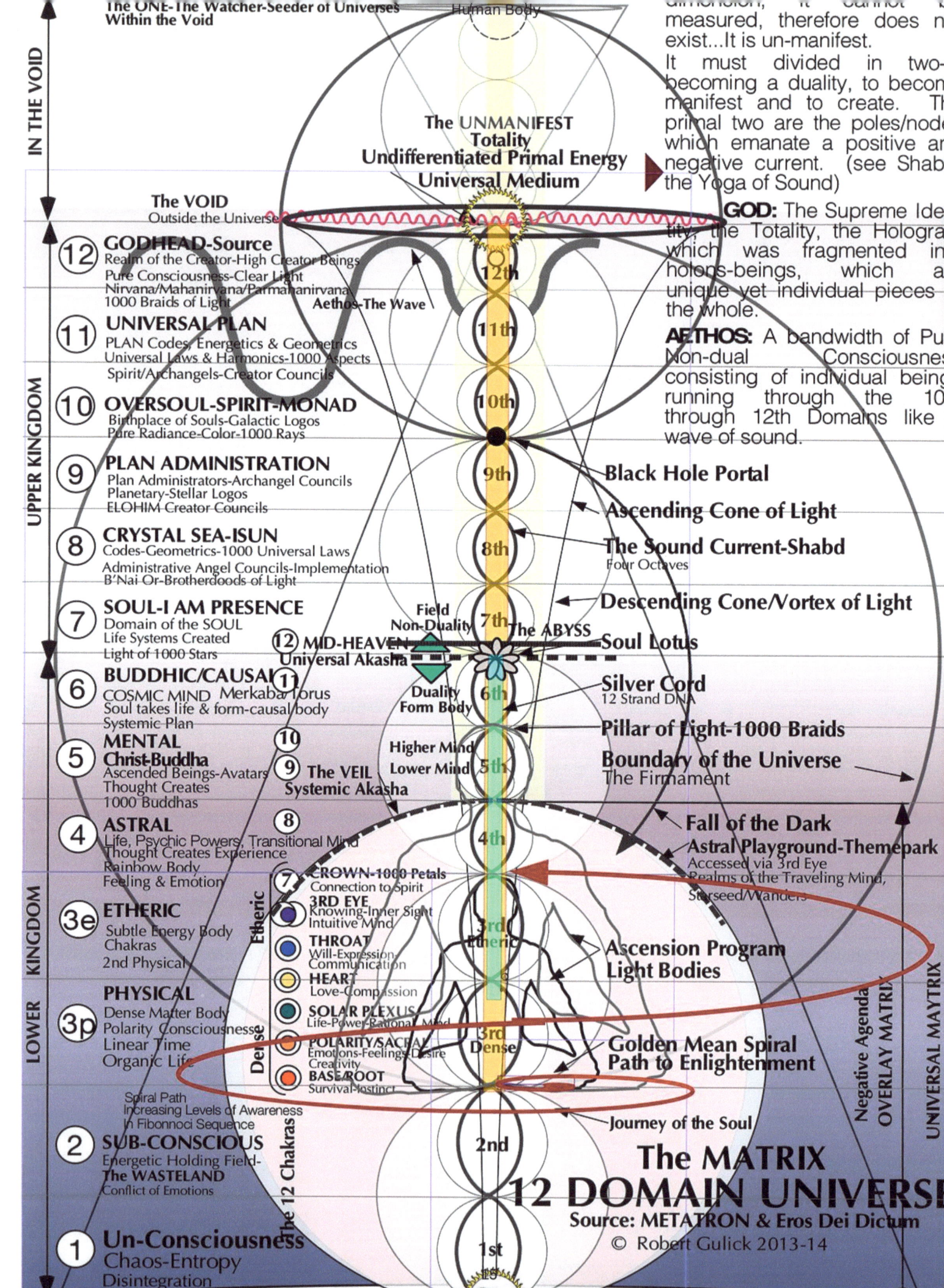

The MATRIX
12 DOMAIN UNIVERSE
Source: METATRON & Eros Dei Dictum
© Robert Gulick 2013-14

There are endless dimensions and densitites within the dimensions that we can potentially interact with. This chart shows the main ones humans can best perceive.

Reincarnation is real, it was removed from the Bible to keep humanity in fear. On this 3D earth plane we have reincarnated over and over many times. Our soul will keep incarnating again and again and never dies.

It's important to release your fear of dying and to live each life to the fullest. Find out what your soul missions and contracts are.

Not only have you reincarnated before but your soul has also been different types of beings too like animals, plants, rocks, elementals, angels and aliens.

Your soul may not even originate from here. A Starseeds means that your soul comes from another place.

Where are you from?
Why did you incarnate here?

Parasitic entities easily attach and feed off beings that have low vibrations and are unaware of their own consciousness and energy bodies.

They can cause disease, energy drainage, intrusive thoughts, anxiety and overall fear.

You are double if not more powerful than they are. Part of your soul journey here is figuring that out.

When your vibration is high and energy bodies are full & strong. Negative parasitic beings can not attach to you or even come near you as they will transmute.

Say "I cut all cords now" to help release them.

When humans are in a state of fear, we leak Loosh energy from our energetic bodies.

Many parasitic entities feed primarily off of Loosh including Reptilians and Archons. Stop giving your power away to them.

This is an important time in humanity's history where we need to energetically cut off the supply of loosh to the parasitic beings!

The third eye or pineal gland is our gateway into the multidimensional realms, interstellar communication, and travel via our light bodies and psychic abilities.

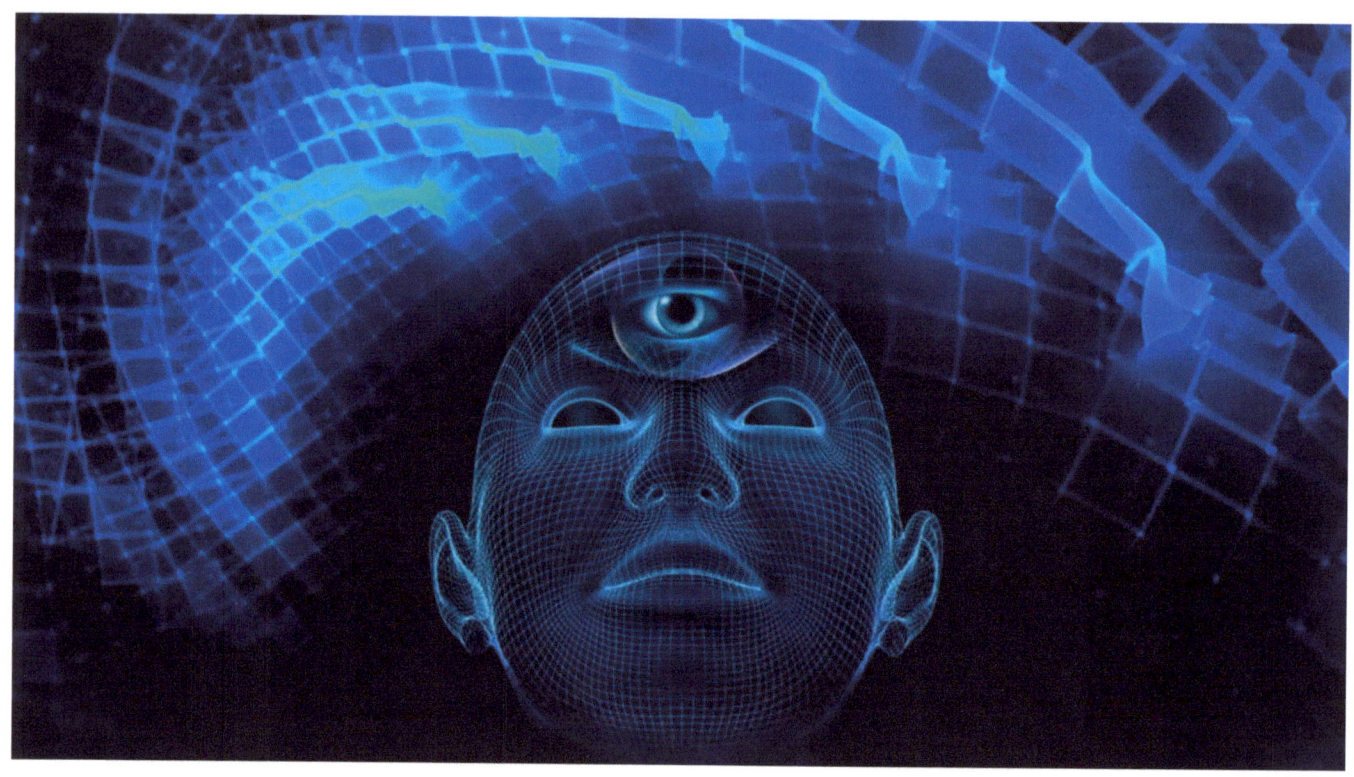

We have many types of extrasensory abilities called Clairs such as clairvoyance, clairsentience, claircognisent, etc. These abilities exist in all humans. We know them better as our gut instinct and spidey sense. They are an extension of our physical abilities that our energetic bodies utilize.

All humans are innately spiritual beings. We are connected through the Cosmic web to the the unlimited pure and loving Source energy.

We all have extrasensory and interdimensional abilities. Yes, we can even levitate as seen here.

Our Earth is not what we've been told and taught to believe. She is like a never ending honeycomb with an inner earth sun and civilizations.

She is a conscious multidimensional feminine being that exists on multiple planes of existence. She is 1D solid, 2D flat, 3D Hallow, and 4D energetic.
As we move into 5D, so does she. Send her love, she needs all the help she can get.

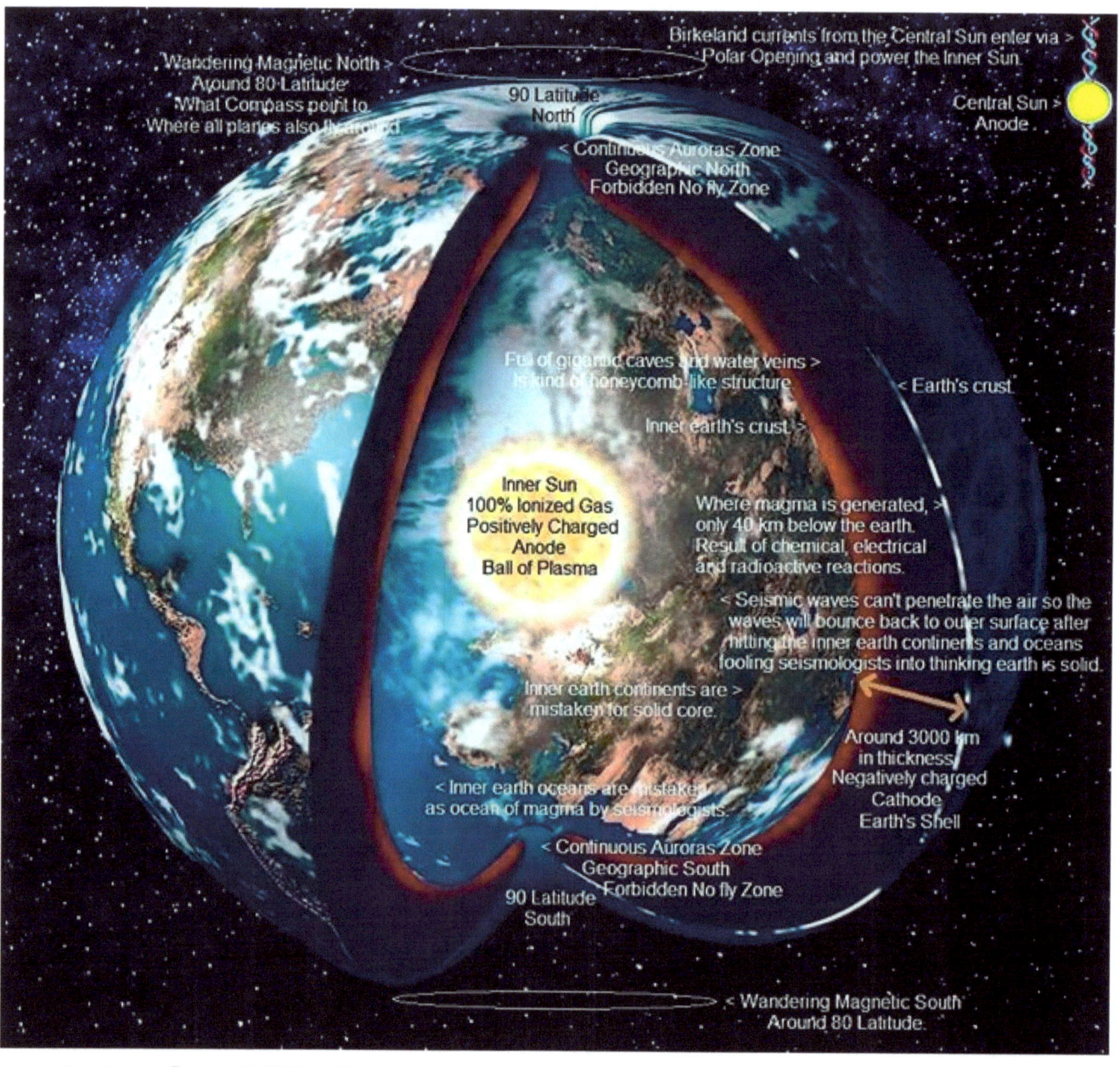

Join the QFT Community to clean up Earth while healing humanity.

There's also infinite alternative realities and we quantum leap between them all the time!

This is called Quantum Jumping. You can master this to create your dream life.

Our souls have reincarnated over and over many times. We often reincarnate with the same souls and ones we have karmic bonds with.

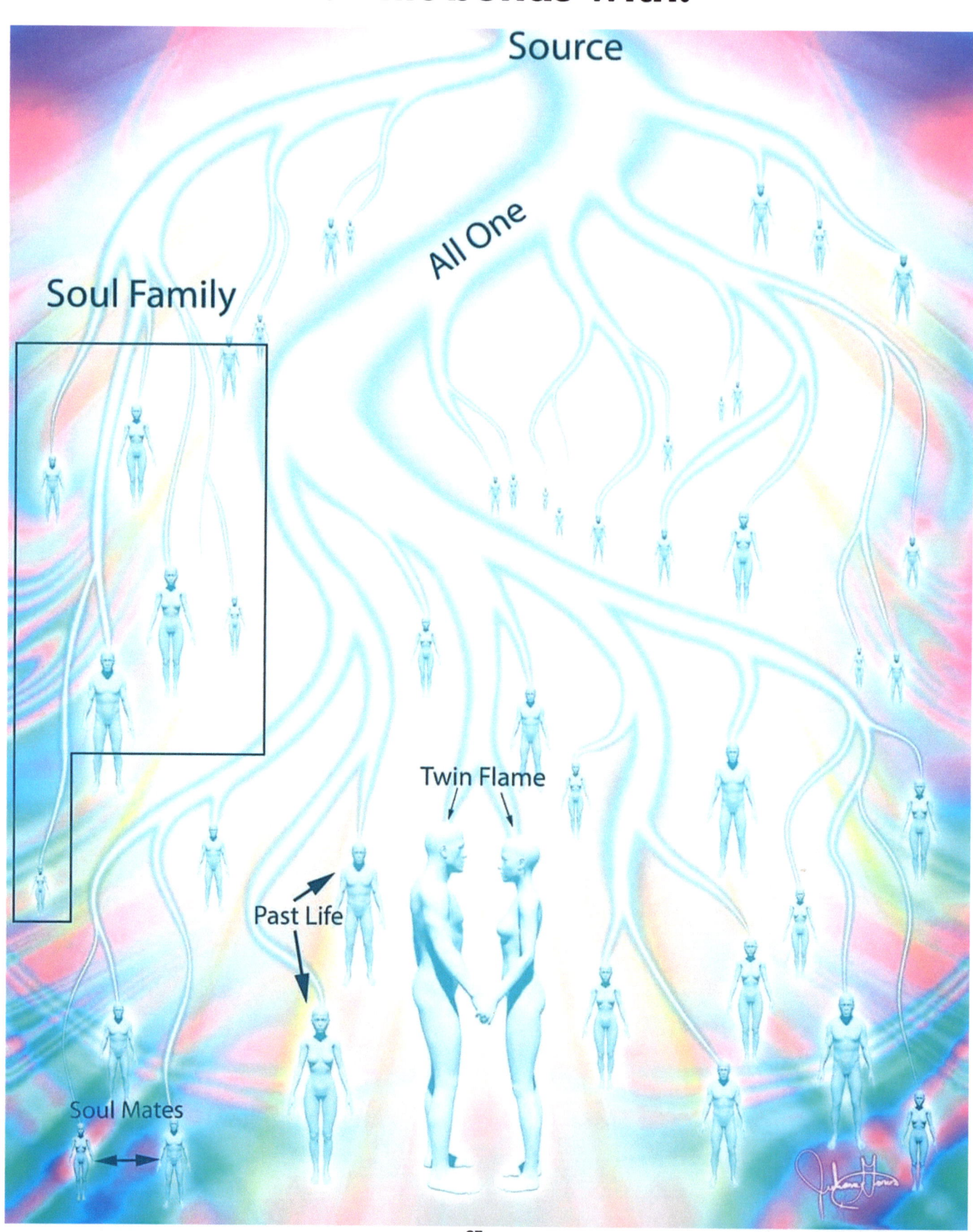

Heaven also known as Nirvana is real and where our soul goes to rest after our physical body dies. You do a life review shortly after passing then go into the resting & reincarnation cycle.

Our Earth has a consciousness, just as we and everything else on this planet and in our universe does too.

There are hidden portals, inner earth tunnels, deep underground bases, underwater cities, and so much more. Flat earth exists, as does Hallow earth, and molten core earth all on separate dimensional planes along with many others. What we know is less than 10% of what the true reality is.

The Earth is riddled with corruption. This image sums up how 99% of people with less money carry the 1% of people that hold 99% of the total wealth.

Notably, The Federal Reserve is not federal at all and is a private company that gets more wealthy from poor people paying interest. Riss Flex is an exceptional woman that's exposing global corruption with extensive undeniable evidence.

The worst of all is the Military Industrial Complex (MIC). It's made up of many different companies and groups that manipulate the world economics, politics, religions, media, etc. All to benefit their groups while exploiting humanity.

My upcoming true crime book title called "They" will deep dive into all of this.

Our earth has split timelines between 3D and 5D...and places in between 4D.

Are you intentionally choosing your reality? If not, then who is?

Now is the time to become fully aware of your consciousness, take control of your mind, reprogram your RAS and align to your soul missions.

There is an etheric Cosmic web that exists throughout the whole universe, through our earth, and each of us. It connects us all together. It is physically represented by the fascia webbing throughout our bodies.

This is the key to exploring the universe. We can travel through this in the astral plane and with our psychic abilities. You can channel information from beings and from the collective consciousness. You will learn about this and much more in my next book "How to Contact Aliens".

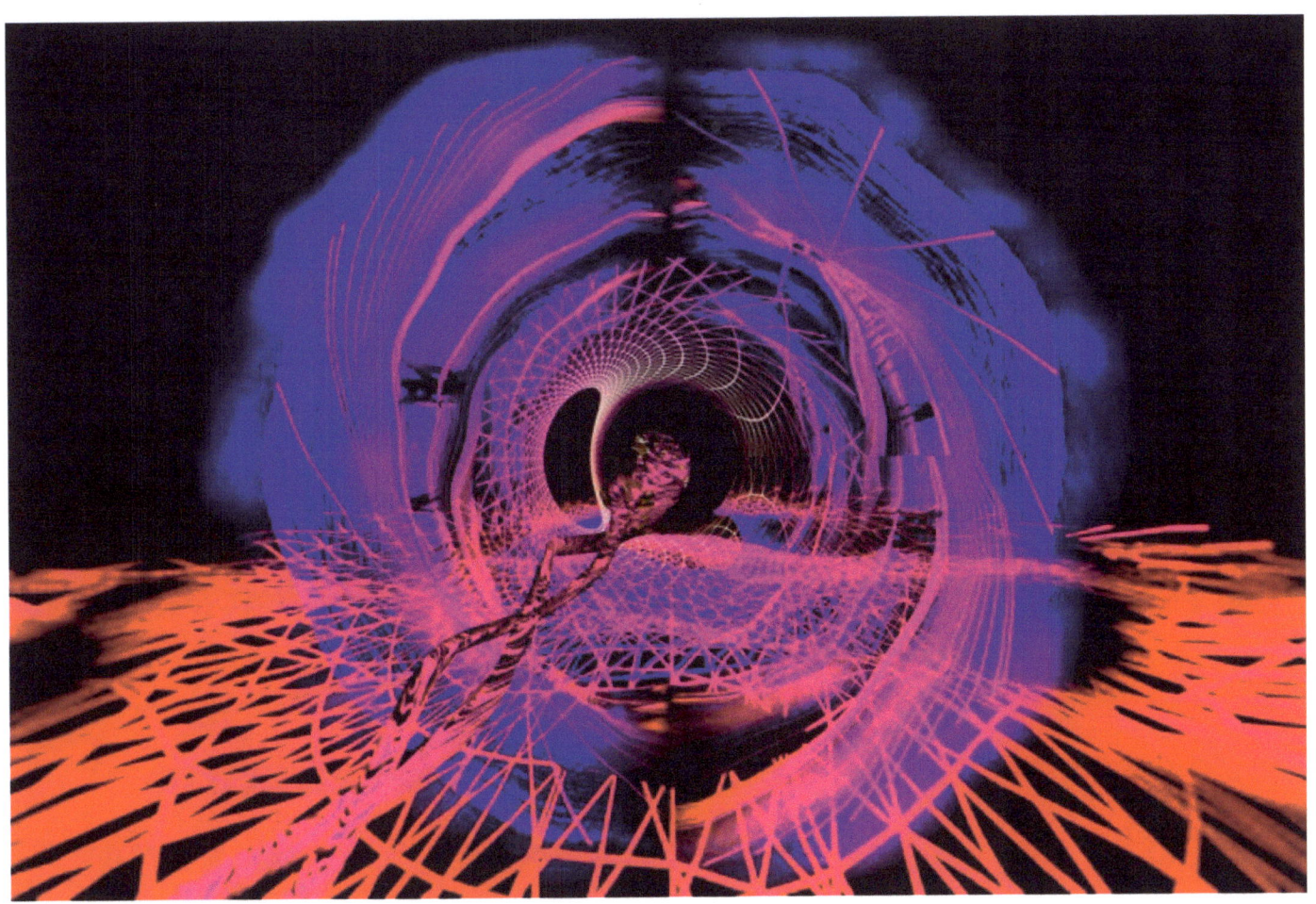

Humanity is a divine creation and we have the ability to divinely co-create our reality with God.

The devil or luciferians that believe themselves separate from God cannot create. They can only pervert and twist.

These are the 12 main universal laws that our Universe operates in.

Humanity is in the biggest shift in consciousness.

Which side are you on?
The light or the dark? And, why?

What is your higher purpose in this?
We all have one and yours is important!

All Alien beings know God and Jesus. I will discuss more on this and how everything is divinely connected in my next book 'God, Jesus, & Aliens'.

Star Beings

Star Beings, aliens, ETs, Celestials, etc. have always been here on earth hiding, cloaking, and disguising themselves - many pretend to be human. They are very real and aware of much more than we are. We share DNA with between 22-24 different types of them and are considered as "cosmic cousins". The vast majority of them are benevolent and want to connect and help humanity once we have raised our vibrational consciousness into 5D. The malevolent ones are parasitic, they feed off of human loosh and don't want us to ascend into higher consciousness. It's ultimately up to humanity to rise above or be stuck in the matrix until the Solar Flash occurs.

There are thousands of different types of beings that interact with Earth. Roughly thirty main ones mostly interact with humanity and of those four types are attempting to maintain control over humanity.

There are billions of worlds and friendly beings of higher intelligence that we can connect with and learn so much from.

They all know God and Jesus, along with many other ascended masters. Humanity has needed all this time up until now to consciously evolve on our own. They are making contact individually now, get ready!

Spirit Guides

Everyone has spirit guides helping them through this incarnation to help progress your soul. If you need help on your soul journey I highly recommend going inward through meditation and allowing your guides to help you. See my resources for additional people to help you on your journey.

This is a photo of ET beings at a Dr. Greer CE5 event that is focused Human to ET communication through oneness consciousness meditation.

There are millions of groups with billions of people making contact. Notible groups are on Dr. Greer's CE5 app and ET Let's Talk by Kosta Makreas.

The Shady Grey Deal

After the Roswell Crash in 1947, the Zeta Reticuli Grey's made a deal with the US Military to exchange advanced technology for the use of humans without their recollection or harm.

They've abducted billions of people without their knowledge and did cause harm to many. They bred with them without their knowledge. It's very common for Starseeds to have hybrid children and not know it. Any people that spoke against this were gaslit with the term they coined "conspiracy theorists" and is still used to this day.

Why did the Zeta's do this? They were dying off because they had cloned themselves too many times and needed humans to help repopulate their people.

Unfortunately, humanity didn't get to make that decision as the US Military Industrial Complex did for us. They used humanity in secret, hoarded all advanced technology for themselves, trillions of US Tax payer dollars for their projects while humanity suffered. No more hiding this now!

Grey-Human Hybrid Essasani Beings

These are Grey-Human Hybrid beings called the Essasani and Sassani.

Chances are high you have some of these hybrid offspring!

Suppressed Advanced Technology

This quantum technology was traded for the use of humans and has been used here for decades. We are capable of switching everything to free energy, healing all humans, and the planet. Every major industry would be disrupted which is why over 6000s patents are being surpressed.

Dr. Greer's latest film "The Lost Century" goes through this in great detail.

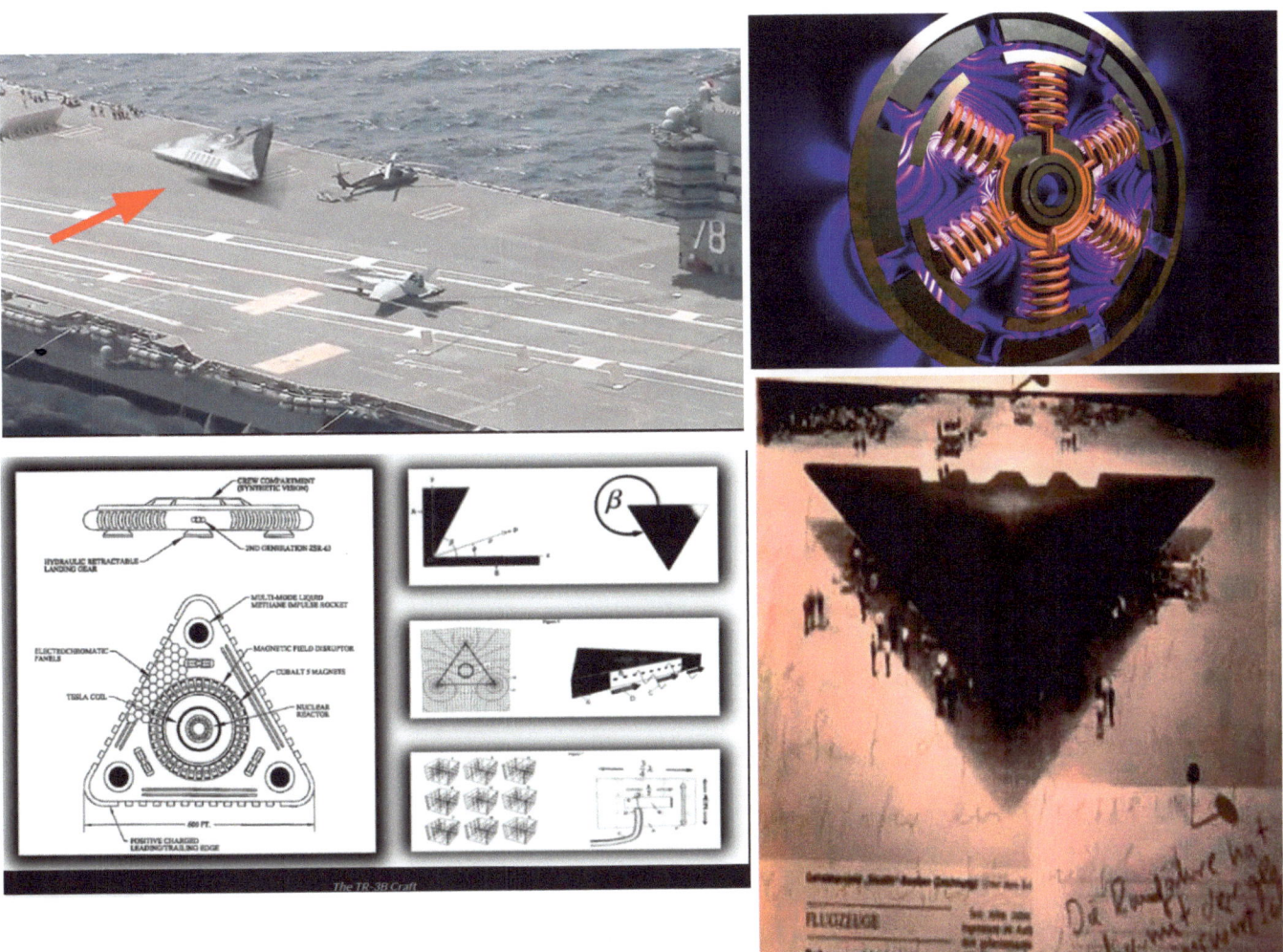

The facts of the matter are this. The technology to heal every ailment and cure every disease exists. Technology exists that can de-age humans. We could increase our lifespans by hundreds to even thousands of years. All the technology we need to completely wipe out poverty, pollution, climate issues, while providing homes and food for everyone and for the world to thrive peacefully. It's already here, it's just not fully disclosed yet.

All of this information has been hidden and suppressed. Because it would destroy the corrupt evil system that's running the military industrial complex. They are the main group hiding and hoarding all of this technology so fearful suffering (Loosh energy) can continue.

This is coming to an end now. Humanity has awakened and we refuse to be slaves any longer.

Say this out loud with passion:

I am a sovereign cosmic being. I now take full control of my consciousness and vibration. I am whole, complete & ascending into 5th dimension consciousness.

Next are some of the great awakening maps to help evolve your understanding of true health, wellness and the reality of what's occurred here.

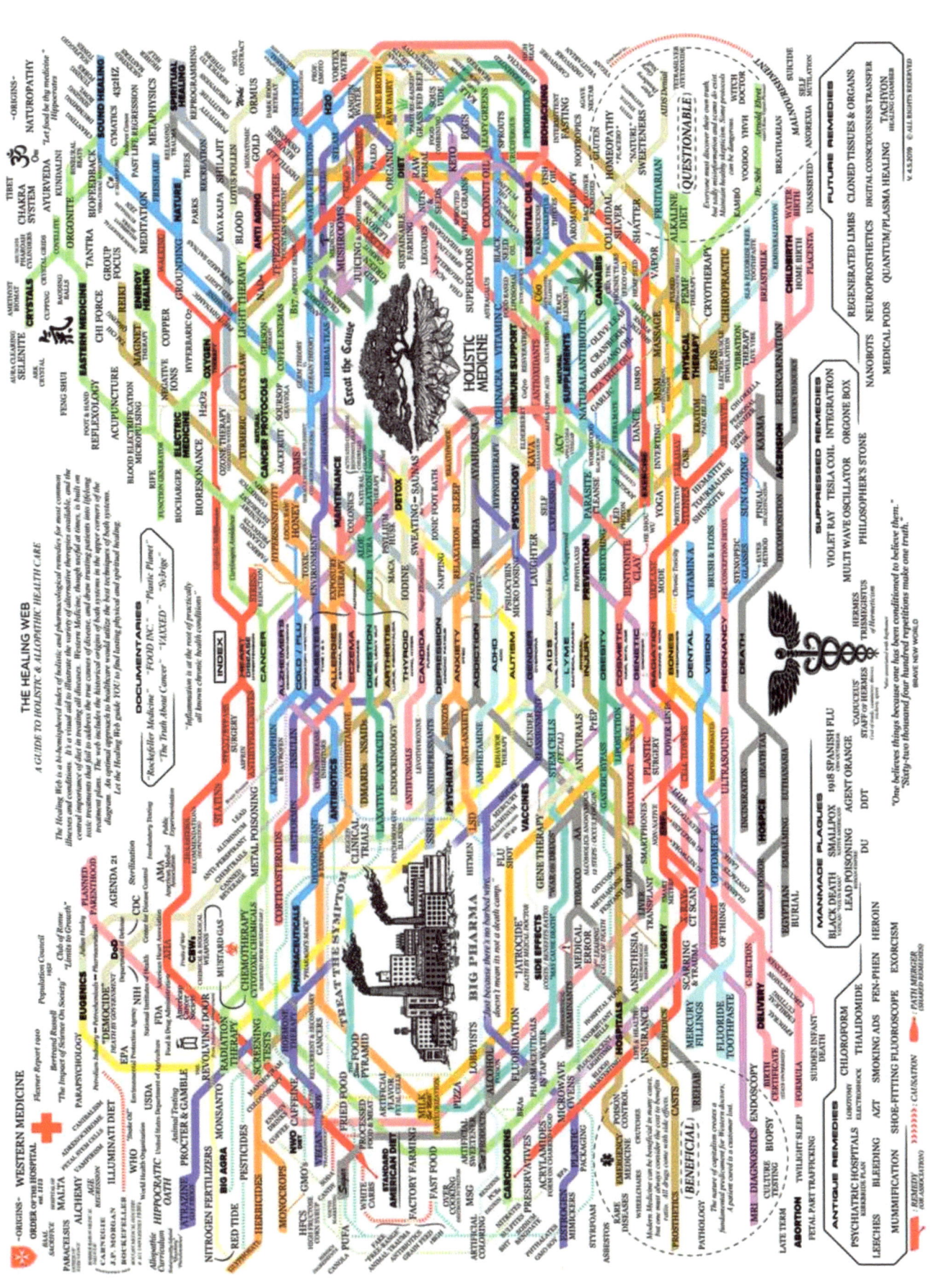

At some point, there will be a great solar flash that will occur and a pole shift. To be ready for this, humanity needs to activate their light bodies and higher consciousness.

Notable People Worth Researching

Dr. Steven Greer

Founder of the Full Disclosure movement and CE5 human to ET contact.

Dr. Salvatore Pias

Inventor of the HAUC and many other quantum advanced technologies patented by the US Navy.

Billy Carson

Theologian, historian and cosmic knowledge guide for humanity. Founder of Forbidden knowledge.

Dr. Salvatore Pais

Kosta Makreas

Founder of ET Let's Talk with millions of members worldwide and ongoing in person and online events.

RA The Law of One

A highly advanced social memory complex that answers the deepest of universal questions.

Dr. Jose Silva

Founder of the Silva Method, it's the way to alter your brain waves into Alpha for super human learning & abilities.

Dolores Cannon

Author, speaker, and founder of QHHT Hypnotherapy and past life regression.

Dr. Joe Dispenza

Author and founder of Brain and Heart Coherence Meditation for 5D healing.

Louise Hay

Author and founder of Cognitive Thought Therapy. You Can Heal Your Life!

Corey Goode

Former Secret Space Program (SSP) participant. Author, full disclosure and cosmic knowledge advocate.

David Wilcock

Theologian, historian, author, full disclosure, ET, and Angelic informant.

Emery Smith

Former SSP, cosmic knowledge informant and host.

Debz Shakti

Quantum hypnotherapist, lifelong contactee, channeler, and health & life coach.

Sharma Pillay

Reptilian attachment specialist & cosmic knowledge activator.

Elizabeth April

GFL contact. Fully activated starseed that shares cosmic knowledge.

Riss Flex

Independent Researcher & Reporter on global corruption by elites, government officials, and much more.

Bashar

Darryl Anka channels a being named Bashar that explains the universe and answers human questions.

Spirit Science

The best animated series explaining practically everything!

References & Links

- Page 1: String theory: https://medium.com/@paulaustinmurphy2000/do-you-realise-just-how-tiny-strings-are-46fdc136ef6f
- Page 2: Higgs Boson God Particle https://sayostudio.com/higgs-boson/
- Page 4: pictures: Spirit Science has complete full ancient wisdom and cosmic knowledge of pretty much everything discussed here and more!
    - https://www.spiritsciencecentral.com/
- Page 5: Reiki chakra image from https://reikiscoop.com/
- Page 6: Human toroidal field: https://www.cosmic-core.org/free/article-101b-science-aether-units-part-5-the-torus-cosmometry/
- Page 7: All toroidal fields: https://i.pinimg.com/originals/ad/81/99/ad81999d8994427e9d28b813665a4baf.jpg
- Page 8: Universal Life Force Currents https://i.pinimg.com/736x/06/70/25/06702504ae76f59e76b661e3310035fe.jpg
- Page 9: Human Brain Waves https://pogledi.net/
- Page 10: Human Brain Canva.com
- Page 11: Dimensions Vibrations & Colors: https://www.actualized.org/forum/topic/81999-disgust-in-loc/
- Page 12: Map of Consciousness by David Hawkins https://i.pinimg.com/736x/25/d2/26/25d226e5523af519377b68fe7d369d84.jpg
- Page 13: Ways to Raise Your Vibration by HealingFacts https://i.pinimg.com/736x/3f/6e/af/3f6eafb2e9e2ec701138a7c3ce58bb27.jpg
- Page 14: Dimensions https://christosavatar.com/
- Page 15: Dimensional Matrix http://mind-matrix.net/wp-content/uploads/2018/07/12-domain-universe.jpg
- Page 16: Spiritual Ascension https://www.instagram.com/p/CFAScTuHo3z/?igshid=10w2egw7uo5m4&epik=dj0yJnU9TkVUdmV6UWYxbG05YlJCX0tCUkxGeHE4bHczZlFjUDMmcD0wJm49cVVqdUFudGJWR1FWZmUzZldrdmhfQSZ0PUFBQUFBR1FLWEY4
- Page 17: Reincarnation: https://buddhaweekly.com/wp-content/uploads/2015/12/Reincarnation-illustration.jpg
- Page 18: Reincarnation: https://miro.medium.com/v2/resize:fit:900/1*WXWR_ldDlS7rYlTR37mpbg.jpeg
- Page 19 & 20: Entity Attachment https://fractalenlightenment.com/35625/spirituality/the-impact-of-negative-entities-on-our-aura-getting-rid-of-them/attachment/aura-cleansing-negative-entity
- Page 21: Loosh Farm https://science-spirituelle.com/quest-ce-quune-ferme-energetique-loosh/
- Page 22: Loosh https://beforeitsnews.com/contributor/upload/29329/images/loosh%20vinctum.jpg
- Page 23: Canva.com
- Page 24: Humans Levitating: Kid Monk https://i.pinimg.com/originals/d9/0f/0b/d90f0b8eb4e66dd61bb3c3a5e0ff4aec.jpg
- Page 24: Man Monk levitating https://www.youtube.com/watch?v=Y6Owljucs00

References & Links

- Page 25: Inner Earth https://www.meuselwitz-guss.de/tag/craftshobbies/is-the-earth-hollow.php
- Page 26: ET Worlds https://exoplanets.nasa.gov/resources/42/rocky-terrestrial-worlds/
- Page 27: Soul Family https://www.julianagarcesart.com/product/soul-streams/
- Page 28: Heaven https://afkimel.wordpress.com/2020/05/03/slowly-reading-st-athanasius-those-pesky-dualists/
- Page 29: Antarctica https://www.retreet.org/blog/tag/Antarctica
- Page 30: Capitalism https://www.fool.com/investing/general/2015/06/11/robber-barons-the-definition-of-the-dark-side-of-c.aspx
- Page 31: Parallel Universes https://www.indiatimes.com/news/world/parallel-universes-do-exist-and-are-already-reaching-out-to-us-scientists-confirm-266390.html
- Page 32: Portal https://www.thetimes.co.uk/article/clyde-tunnel-becomes-a-work-of-art-fqc8gvgkv
- Page 33: Creation https://open.spotify.com/album/4vYyba18zQEzPd5TcggbxT
- Page 34: 12 Universal Laws https://www.facebook.com/TheGoddess.Guidance7/photos/a.103078444975522/158773789405987/?paipv=0&eav=AfYhX60a6MpPf-ZZPdS6pKx86uFp85sEcvP6pneZZwYAP_X5_MBvTSAWxEPrXbO3sSM
- Page 35: War https://www.beyondthebrokendoor.com/the-revolving-door/
- Page 36: ETs https://www.deviantart.com/vervex/art/Extraterrestrial-potraits-310825876
- Page 37: Aliens landed https://www.deviantart.com/matjosh/art/Told-You-So-731746498
- Page 38: 1st picture: https://indianinthemachine.wordpress.com/category/the-galactic-federation-of-light-and-sananda-our-returned-master-teacher/
- Page 38: 2nd picture https://www.pinterest.ca/pin/700239442035692113/
- Page 39: Spirit Guides https://www.booksie.com/527118-our-world-in-transition-chapter-58
- Page 40: CE5 ET Contact https://siriusdisclosure.com/apps/
- Page 41: Grey Alien https://www.amazon.ca/Extraterrestrial-Species-Almanac-Ultimate-Reptilians/dp/1590033043
- Page 41: Alien Abduction https://nocturnalrevelries.com/tag/alien-abduction/
- Page 42: Alien Abduction https://www.pinterest.ca/pin/702631979349604756/
- Page 43: Essasani https://www.pinterest.ca/pin/280912095487815743/
- Page 44: Triangle UFO https://newsmedia.tasnimnews.com/Tasnim/Uploaded/Image/1397/06/24/13970624120104161536534.jpg

References & Links

- Page 44: Coil Motor https://www.ecdrives.com/engineering/ec-technology.html
- Page 44: Space craft http://calameo.download/00041324170431f73c2b3
- Page 44: TR-b3 space craft https://twitter.com/Fortean777/status/1532768483557412864
- Page 46, 47 & 48 https://greatawakeningreport.com/the-big-picture/
- Page 49: Dr. Greer https://siriusdisclosure.com/
- Page 49: Dr. Salvatore Pais Hauc Patent https://patents.google.com/patent/US10144532B2/en
- Page 49: Billy Carson https://www.4biddenknowledge.com/
- Page 50: Kosta Makreas https://etletstalk.com/
- Page 50: The Law of One RA https://www.lawofone.info/
- Page 50: Jose Silva https://silvamethod.com/
- Page 51: Dolores Cannon https://dolorescannon.com/
- Page 51: Dr. Joe Dispenza https://drjoedispenza.com/
- Page 51: Louise Hay https://www.louisehay.com/
- Page 52: Corey Goode https://coreygoode.com/
- Page 52: David Wilcock https://divinecosmos.com/about-david/
- Page 52: Emery Smith https://www.gaia.com/person/emery-smith
- Page 53: Sharma Pillay https://shematsystems.com/
- Page 53: Debz Shakti https://www.debzshakti.com/
- Page 53: Elizabeth April https://elizabethapril.com/
- Page 54: Riss Flex https://rissflex.com/
- Page 54: Bashar by Darryl Anka https://www.bashar.org/
- Page 54: Spirit Science https://www.spiritsciencecentral.com/

Questions to Ask Yourself About Your Beliefs & Paradigm

What are you questioning most?

What do you already know to be true?

Why do you believe the things you do?

What age were you when you learnt them? And, from whom?

What else did you learn at that age that turned out to not be true? See any correlations?

What are your gifts and how best can you share them to help with the consciousness shift?

What life do you want for yourself and humanity?

Breathing & Awareness Exercise

Sit in a quiet place. Take 3 deep breathes in through your nose and out your mouth. Hold your breath after inhaling for 3 seconds before exhaling.

What do you notice in your body?

Now, take 3 more deep breaths but this time put your hands on your heart.
What do you notice now?

Take 3 more deep breaths, this time close your eyes and imagine the air coming into your body is bright cleansing light and the air coming out is removing dark toxins from all of your cells.

What do you notice now?

Try this each day to grow your energetic awareness.

Lisa M. is a clairvoyant mystic contactee, abductee, and experiencer of many different types of extraterrestrials and interdimensionals.

In 2019, two Reptilian beings showed up in her room in the middle of the night trying to make her an offer. She turned them down and three weeks later two high vibrational beings came to her with a long list of things she needed to accomplish. A few months later the 'coco' broke out and the world as she knew it was long gone. She started a CE5 group and met people who were also abducted and had ET experiences. She continues to have contact and is determined to raise the vibration of humanity while sharing advanced cosmic knowledge. Here are her upcoming titles and be sure to find her on TikTok at 5DLIFENOW.

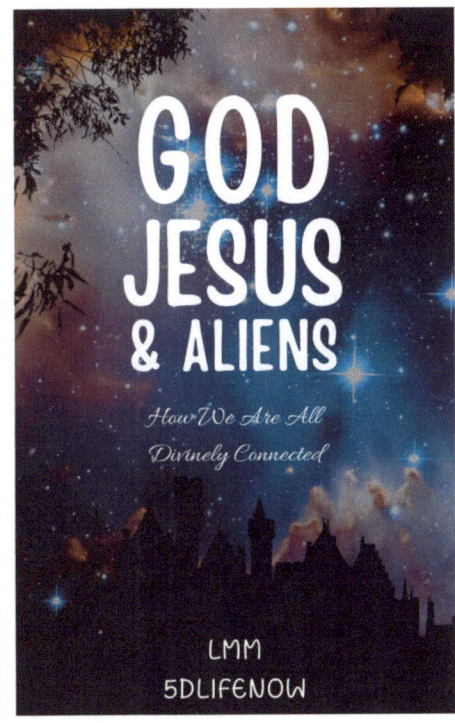

5D Consciousness Activations

"The Great Remembering of Humanity"

In this 5D Consciousness Activation Guidebook you will learn about the human body, earth, universe, Star Beings, Great Awakening Maps system, all the references you need to learn more and bonus exercises and tips along the way.

By reading this book, you're taking a giant leap into cosmic knowledge that has been hidden from humanity for dark and light reasons. Congratulations on making it this far in your soul journey. You are well on your 5D development.

LMM
5DLIFENOW